THE HOUSE RULES
(OR "HOW TO SURVIVE LIVING TOGETHER") BOOK

- ✓ WANT PEACE AT HOME?
- ✓ WANT THINGS YOUR WAY?

YOU NEED THIS BOOK!

spruce

FRANCESCA LEUNG

For Alex and John, who always put up with me.
And Mom, Dad, Vin, and Sarah—thanks you guys, got there in the end.

An Hachette UK Company
www.hachette.co.uk

First published in Great Britain in 2015 by Spruce,
a division of Octopus Publishing Group Ltd
Carmelite House
50 Victoria Embankment
London EC4Y 0DZ
www.octopusbooksusa.com

Distributed in the US by
Hachette Book Group
1290 Avenue of the Americas
4th and 5th Floors
New York, NY 10020

Distributed in Canada by
Canadian Manda Group
664 Annette St.
Toronto, Ontario, Canada M6S 2C8

ISBN 978 1 84601 505 2

Printed and bound in China

10 9 8 7 6 5 4 3 2 1

DISCLAIMER

THE AUTHOR AND THE PUBLISHER TAKE NO RESPONSIBILITY FOR ANY DISPUTES AND ARGUMENTS THAT WILL INEVITABLY ARISE AS A RESULT OF USING THIS BOOK. THEY DO, HOWEVER, CLAIM CREDIT FOR ANY SUCCESS STORIES AND PEACE KEPT AS A RESULT OF USING THIS BOOK. YOU ARE MOST WELCOME.

Contents

INTRODUCTION

Divas, drama queens, slobs, and stubborn passive-aggressive types—we've all lived with them and, more importantly, we're all guilty of being them. But there are also the saints who make us a cup of coffee just the way we like it, or the ones who really love cleaning (what freaks...).

Most problems that arise in shared households are caused by assuming another person is somehow psychic and knows how you like things done. However, unless you're living with Professor Xavier, this will sadly not be possible. But this isn't about changing people, it's about compromising—so here is a book designed to make everyone's life a little bit easier.

Each section is based on a room of the house, with a miscellaneous section at the back for more general rules. Simply make your way through the book, filling in your preferences (there is space on each page for additional comments), then hand it over to the long-suffering people you live with to refer to and add to at their leisure.(Now, obviously there will still be disagreements over the right way to do things, but if anyone disagrees with you, you wrote it down first.)

So whether it's a question of letting the faucet run when washing dishes, or the ongoing debate about which way the toilet paper should face on the holder, you've got your policy down in writing.

... and so it begins.

CHAPTER 1: KITCHEN

Do you speak coffee?
EDUCATE YOUR HOUSEHOLD AND STATE YOUR COFFEE OF CHOICE

☐ **AMERICANO**
HOT WATER +
ESPRESSO

☐ **CAPPUCCINO**
ESPRESSO + HOT
MILK + STEAMED
MILK FOAM

☐ **CHAI LATTE**
SPICED TEA +
STEAMED MILK
+ ESPRESSO

☐ **ESPRESSO**
CONCENTRATED
COFFEE

☐ **FLAT WHITE**
DOUBLE ESPRESSO
+ HOT MILK + A LITTLE
BIT OF MILK FOAM

☐ **ICED COFFEE**
COFFEE + ICE

☐ **IRISH COFFEE**
IRISH WHISKEY +
CREAM + COFFEE

☐ **LATTE**
ESPRESSO +
STEAMED MILK

☐ **MACCHIATO**
ESPRESSO + DASH
OF MILK FOAM

☐ **MOCHA**
ESPRESSO + STEAMED
MILK + CHOCOLATE

OTHER / COFFEE RUN FOR OTHER PEOPLE:

The Coffee Chart

☐ VERY AU LAIT

☐ MILKY

☐ BARELY A HIT OF COFFEE

☐ COFFEE-SHORTAGE

☐ WARM-ME-UP COFFEE

☐ PARIS CAFE IN THE SPRINGTIME

☐ GET THROUGH THE DAY

☐ SERIOUS BUSINESS

☐ STILL HUNGOVER

☐ ALL-NIGHTER

OTHER PEOPLE'S PREFERENCES:

Coffee fanatic

BOILING / COFFEE PRESS / VACUUM BREWER / DRIP BREW / COLD BREW / ESPRESSO MACHINE / STOVE-TOP POT / INSTANT

TYPE OF COFFEE:
BRAND:_____
COUNTRY:_____
BLEND:_____

☐ BLACK

MILK:
☐ SKIM
☐ 2 PERCENT
☐ WHOLE
☐ HALF AND HALF
☐ SOY
☐ ALMOND

☐ HOT
☐ COLD
☐ FROTHY

SUGAR:
☐ SWEETENER
☐ NONE
☐ 1 SUGAR
☐ 2 SUGARS
☐ 3 SUGARS
☐ 4+ SUGARS

☐ PACKETS
☐ CUBES
☐ TEASPOONS
☐ HEAPED TEASPOONS
   –NONE OF THIS TINY
   SPOONS NONSENSE

SERVED WITH:
☐ CHOCOLATE
☐ A COOKIE
☐ A CIGARETTE
☐ A SMILE

OTHER REQUIREMENTS:
_____
_____
_____
_____

8

Anyone for tea?

☐ I DON'T DRINK TEA

☐ EARL GREY
☐ ENGLISH BREAKFAST
☐ DARJEELING
☐ ASSAM
☐ CHAI

☐ GREEN
☐ WHITE
☐ JASMINE
☐ OOLONG
☐ LAPSANG SOUCHONG
☐ MATCHA

☐ ROOIBOS
☐ CHAMOMILE
☐ MINT
☐ LEMON & GINGER
☐ FRUIT
☐ OTHER:_____

BRAND:_____

TEA SHOULD ALWAYS BE SERVED:
☐ HOT
☐ CHILLED
☐ WITH PLENTY OF ICE CUBES

☐ DECAFFEINATED
☐ BAGS
☐ LEAVES

FOR LEAVES:
☐ STRAINED (TAKE THEM OUT)
☐ INFUSED (LEAVE THEM IN)

☐ TEAPOT, ALL-OUT, LET'S DO THIS

OPTIMAL STEEPING TIME:___ MINUTES

9

The art of tea

MILK:
- [ ] NONE, THE FLAVOR OF TEA IS ALL I NEED
- [ ] SKIM, AKA REALLY WATERY MILK
- [ ] 2 PERCENT, AKA WATERY MILK
- [ ] WHOLE, THIS IS MILK
- [ ] GOAT'S MILK, BECAUSE COW IS NOT THE ONLY ANIMAL
- [ ] SOY, AKA BEAN WATER
- [ ] ALMOND. MADE FROM ALMONDS

- [ ] MILK FIRST (SHAKES HEAD)
- [ ] MILK LAST (SO YOU CAN GET THE COLOR RIGHT. IT'S LOGICAL)

SUGAR:
- [ ] SWEETENER, ACTUALLY
- [ ] NONE
- [ ] 1 SUGAR
- [ ] 2 SUGARS
- [ ] 3 SUGARS
- [ ] 4+ SUGARS

- [ ] PACKETS
- [ ] CUBES
- [ ] TEASPOONS
- [ ] HEAPED TEASPOONS

OTHER REQUESTS:
_____
_____

LEMON?
- [ ] YES, PLEASE
- [ ] WHAT? NO

10

The Tea Chart

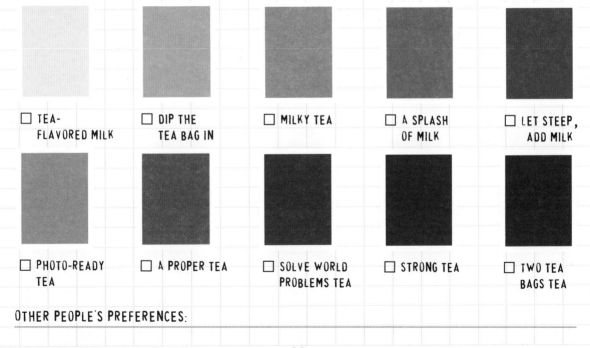

☐ TEA-FLAVORED MILK
☐ DIP THE TEA BAG IN
☐ MILKY TEA
☐ A SPLASH OF MILK
☐ LET STEEP, ADD MILK

☐ PHOTO-READY TEA
☐ A PROPER TEA
☐ SOLVE WORLD PROBLEMS TEA
☐ STRONG TEA
☐ TWO TEA BAGS TEA

OTHER PEOPLE'S PREFERENCES:

Chinaware

☐ MUG
☐ CUP

MY FAVORITE MUG/CUP LOOKS LIKE THIS:

IT IS MY FAVORITE MUG/CUP BECAUSE:

IF YOU BREAK IT, I WILL:
☐ FORCE YOU TO GET ME AN EXACT REPLICA
☐ GET YOU TO BUY ME AN EVEN BETTER ONE
  (A NEAR IMPOSSIBLE TASK)
☐ GIVE YOU A WITHERING LOOK
  TO END ALL WITHERING LOOKS
☐ NOT BE RESPONSIBLE FOR MY ACTIONS
☐ DO NOTHING, FOR I AM MERCIFUL

Favorite cookie

☐ CHOCOLATE CHIP   ☐ SHORTBREAD
☐ OATMEAL RAISIN   ☐ WAFER
☐ PEANUT BUTTER   ☐ SUGAR COOKIE
☐ SNICKERDOODLES   ☐ FORTUNE COOKIE
☐ GINGERBREAD   ☐ OTHER: _____
☐ BISCOTTI

WHAT DO YOU ADVOCATE?
☐ DUNKING
☐ NOT DUNKING

WHAT IS THE BEST COOKIE TO DUNK?

HOW LONG SHOULD YOU DUNK FOR?

OTHER DEMANDS:
_____
_____

12

Alternative hot beverage?

☐ HOT CHOCOLATE
PREFERRED BRAND:_____
NUMBER OF PACKETS /TEASPOONS /HEAPED
TEASPOONS:_____
MADE WITH HOT WATER /MILK. TYPE:_____
ADDED SUGAR?_____

WITH BONUS:
☐ WHIPPED CREAM
☐ MINI MARSHMALLOWS
☐ BIG MARSHMALLOWS
☐ DUSTING OF COCOA
☐ CINNAMON
☐ NUTMEG
☐ OTHER:_____

☐ OTHER HOT DRINK: _____

Variation on the milk theme?

WHEN MILK ALONE JUST ISN'T ENOUGH:

☐ CHOCOLATE MILK
☐ STRAWBERRY MILK
☐ BANANA MILKSHAKE
☐ SMOOTHIE WITH MILK

ADDING A FLAVOR OF SOME SORT:
☐ NUTMEG
☐ VANILLA
☐ GINGERBREAD
☐ CINNAMON
☐ SEASONAL FAVORITE
☐ OTHER:_____

OTHER NOTES:
_____
_____
_____

Water

☐ BOTTLED. BRAND: _____
☐ SPARKLING. BRAND: _____
☐ FROM THE FAUCET

WITH:
☐ A SLICE OF LEMON
☐ A SLICE OF LIME
☐ MINT LEAVES

☐ ICE
☐ NO ICE

FILTERED WATER

☐ FILL UP THE WATER PITCHER AFTER YOU USE IT. PLEASE. FOR THE SAKE OF HUMANITY. FILL IT. MAGIC ELVES DON'T DO IT, YOU KNOW. I DO

☐ WE DON'T FILTER OUR DRINKNG WATER. WHAT DOESN'T KILL YOU MAKES YOU STRONGER

OTHER DEMANDS:
_____
_____
_____

Juice

LEGITIMATELY PART OF YOUR BALANCED DIET

☐ PULP
☐ NO PULP

☐ FRESHLY SQUEEZED
☐ FROM CONCENTRATE

FLAVOR:
☐ ORANGE
☐ APPLE
☐ GRAPE
☐ CRANBERRY
☐ GRAPEFRUIT
☐ POMEGRANATE
☐ TROPICAL
☐ LYCHEE
☐ MANGO
☐ PINEAPPLE
☐ TOMATO
☐ OTHER:_____

Soft drinks

OR PROBABLY "MIXERS" IF WE'RE BEING HONEST

SODA:
☐ COLA
☐ CHERRY COLA
☐ GINGER ALE
☐ ROOT BEER
☐ CREAM SODA
☐ LEMON-LIME

STILL:
☐ LEMONADE
☐ COCONUT WATER
☐ ICED TEA (NOTE: NOT PROPER TEA THAT HAS BEEN ICED)

OTHER NOTES:
_____
_____
_____

15

The wine list

RED // WHITE // ROSÉ

☐ SPARKLING
☐ NOT SPARKLING

PREFERENCES:
GRAPE VARIETY: _____
REGION: _____
(PLEASE MARK ON THE MAP)
VINTAGE: _____

PRIORITY:
☐ QUALITY
☐ QUANTITY

OUTLOOK:
☐ GLASS HALF FULL
☐ GLASS HALF EMPTY
☐ HA! THE BOTTLE, PLEASE

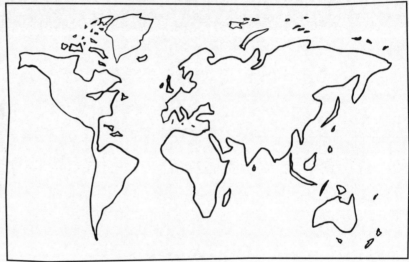

OTHER REQUIREMENTS:
_____
_____

16

Beer color wheel

FANCY A GLASS?

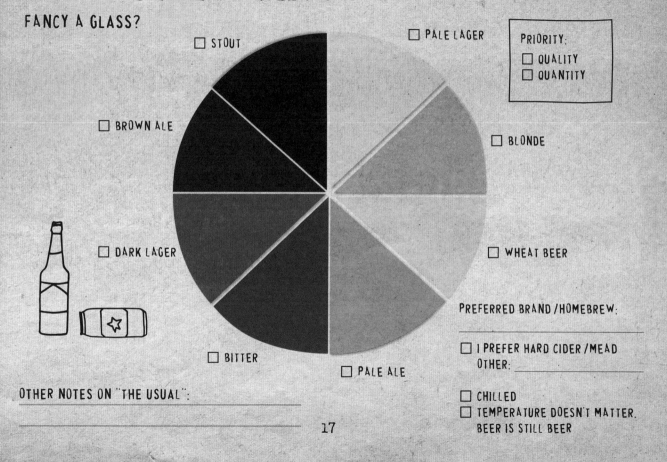

☐ STOUT

☐ PALE LAGER

☐ BROWN ALE

☐ BLONDE

☐ DARK LAGER

☐ WHEAT BEER

☐ BITTER

☐ PALE ALE

PRIORITY:
☐ QUALITY
☐ QUANTITY

PREFERRED BRAND / HOMEBREW:

☐ I PREFER HARD CIDER / MEAD
OTHER: _____

☐ CHILLED
☐ TEMPERATURE DOESN'T MATTER.
BEER IS STILL BEER

OTHER NOTES ON "THE USUAL": _____

17

Happy hour

BASE:
RUM // GIN // VODKA // TEQUILA // MEZCAL // WHISKEY // BRANDY // ABSINTHE // OUZO // SAKE // PORT
OTHER: _____

TYPE:
MARTINI // PINA COLADA // LONG ISLAND ICED TEA // COSMOPOLITAN // MANHATTAN // GIN AND TONIC // OLD FASHIONED //
ZOMBIE // MAI TAI // DAIQUIRI // MOJITO // MARGARITA // WHITE RUSSIAN // SEA BREEZE // SCREWDRIVER // BLOODY MARY
OTHER: _____

STYLE:
ON THE ROCKS // SHAKEN // STIRRED // WITH A SLICE // WITH AN OLIVE // WITH A CHERRY // WITH AN UMBRELLA

And what species are you?

☐ CARNIVORE /
MAINLY MEAT

☐ PESCATARIAN /
FAKE VEGETARIAN /
MEAT WHEN I WANT

☐ OVO-LACTO
VEGETARIAN /
NOTHING WITH A FACE

☐ VEGAN /
TOFU AND SELF-
RIGHTEOUSNESS

☐ FRUITARIAN /
BASICALLY DEAD
OR DYING PLANTS

☐ OMNIVORE / WILL
EAT ANYTHING AND
EVERYTHING IN SIGHT

OTHER DIETARY REQUIREMENTS:
_____
NAME OF CURRENT DIET: _____

ANY FOOD ALLERGIES OR INTOLERANCES?

FIVE FOODS I JUST DON'T LIKE:
1) _____
2) _____
3) _____
4) _____
5) _____

NUT // DAIRY // GLUTEN // SEAFOOD // STRAWBERRIES // SOY // OTHER: _____

Sliced bread, the best thing since bread

RE: Carbohydrates

- ☐ CARBS ARE THE DEVIL! NO CARBS! BREAD MAKES YOU FAT!
- ☐ BREAD IS THE BEST THING THAT EVER HAPPENED TO ME

TYPE:
- ☐ WHITE
- ☐ WHOLE WHEAT
- ☐ SEEDED
- ☐ RYE
- ☐ SOURDOUGH

CUT:
- ☐ THICK SLICE
- ☐ MEDIUM SLICE
- ☐ THIN SLICE
- ☐ TORN OFF THE LOAF, LIKE A BEAST

SHAPE:
- ☐ BAGEL
- ☐ PITA
- ☐ TORTILLA
- ☐ FLATBREAD
- ☐ BAGUETTE
- ☐ NAAN
- ☐ BRIOCHE
- ☐ FOCACCIA
- ☐ SODA
- ☐ CIABATTA
- ☐ PRETZEL

WITH:
- ☐ BUTTER
- ☐ MARGARINE
- ☐ OLIVE OIL DIP
- ☐ CREAM CHEESE
- ☐ PEANUT BUTTER
- ☐ CHOCOLATE SPREAD
- ☐ HUMMUS
- ☐ PATÉ
- ☐ JAM
- ☐ OTHER:_____

OTHER NOTES:

The toast chart

HOW DO YOU LIKE YOUR BREAD COOKED?

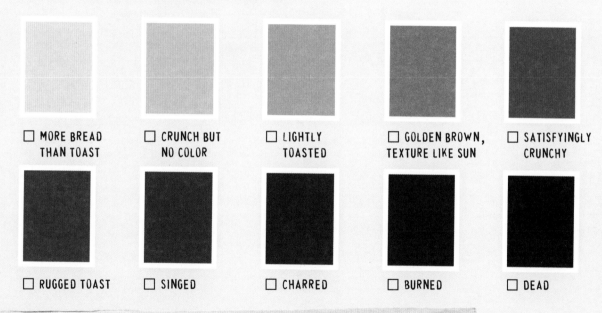

☐ MORE BREAD THAN TOAST

☐ CRUNCH BUT NO COLOR

☐ LIGHTLY TOASTED

☐ GOLDEN BROWN, TEXTURE LIKE SUN

☐ SATISFYINGLY CRUNCHY

☐ RUGGED TOAST

☐ SINGED

☐ CHARRED

☐ BURNED

☐ DEAD

OTHER PEOPLE'S PREFERENCES:

Make me a sandwich

SANDWICH CUTTING:

☐ QUARTERS

☐ DIAGONAL QUARTERS

☐ DIAGONAL HALVES

☐ HALVES LENGTHWISE

☐ WHOLE

☐ CRUSTS ON

☐ CRUSTS OFF

SANDWICH FILLINGS:

CHEESE, CHICKEN, POTATO CHIPS, SLOPPY JOE, SLICED HAM, TURKEY, CHOCOLATE SPREAD, JELLY, PEANUT BUTTER, PB&J, BLT, EGG SALAD, LOX & CREAM CHEESE, TUNA & MAYO, SALAMI, PASTRAMI, BOLOGNA, FALAFEL, HUMMUS, ETC.

A SANDWICH CAN BE A WONDERFUL THING.
PLEASE NAME YOUR TOP 3 SANDWICH FILLINGS:
1) _____
2) _____
3) _____

AND 3 SANDWICH FILLINGS YOU DON'T LIKE:
1) _____
2) _____
3) _____

OTHER DEMANDS:
_____
_____
_____

22

To fridge or not to fridge?

EGGS GO:
- [ ] IN THE FRIDGE, OBVIOUSLY—THERE ARE EVEN EGG HOLDERS THAT THE FRIDGE MAKERS PUT IN
- [ ] NOT IN THE FRIDGE

BREAD GOES:
- [ ] IN THE FRIDGE, TO KEEP IT FRESH
- [ ] NOT IN THE FRIDGE

FRUIT AND TOMATOES GO:
- [ ] IN THE FRIDGE, TO KEEP THEM FRESH
- [ ] NOT IN THE FRIDGE

RE: EXPIRY DATES:
- [ ] AT THE STROKE OF MIDNIGHT ON THE DAY OF THE EXPIRY DATE, THAT FOOD BECOMES INEDIBLE
- [ ] IF IT SMELLS O.K., IT'S O.K.
- [ ] IF IT LOOKS O.K., IT'S O.K.
- [ ] DON'T BE SILLY, YOU CAN SCRAPE THAT MOLD OFF

OTHER WARNINGS / GUIDELINES:
_____

Breakfast of champions

- [ ] EGGS AND BACON
- [ ] CONTINENTAL
- [ ] ASIAN
- [ ] BREAKFAST BURRITO
- [ ] HUEVOS RANCHEROS
- [ ] FRUIT
- [ ] JUICE / SMOOTHIE
- [ ] YOGURT
- [ ] CEREAL / CORNFLAKES
- [ ] MUESLI / GRANOLA
- [ ] PANCAKES
- [ ] WAFFLES
- [ ] OATMEAL
- [ ] CONGEE
- [ ] CEREAL BAR
- [ ] EGGS
- [ ] BAGEL
- [ ] MUFFIN

- [ ] NOTHING

- [ ] OTHER: _____

NOTES: _____
_____

How do you like your eggs in the morning?

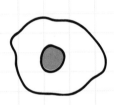

☐ FRIED

☐ OVER EASY

☐ SUNNY SIDE UP

☐ BROKEN YOLK

☐ BOILED

☐ SOFT

☐ MEDIUM

☐ HARD

☐ WITH TOAST

☐ POACHED

☐ BENEDICT

☐ ROYALE

☐ FLORENTINE

☐ **SCRAMBLED**

☐ FLUFFY

☐ BUTTERY

☐ RUNNY

☐ WITH ADDED
   SHELL

☐ **OMELET**

☐ HAM

☐ CHEESE

☐ BELL PEPPERS

☐ **SAUCE**

☐ HOLLANDAISE

☐ KETCHUP

☐ MUSTARD

☐ SALSA

☐ **FRENCH TOAST**

OTHER NOTES:

_____

_____

_____

Pasta shapes

- [ ] THE CLASSIC: SPAGHETTI
- [ ] THE KING OF PASTAS: LINGUINE
- [ ] THE COMFORT BLANKET: LASAGNA
- [ ] THE STRIP: TAGLIATELLE
- [ ] THE TUBE: CANNELLONI
- [ ] THE SOUP HOLDERS: CONCHIGLIE
- [ ] THE TWIST: FUSILLI
- [ ] THE STAPLE: PENNE
- [ ] THE CHEESE ONE: MACARONI
- [ ] THE PACKAGES: RAVIOLI
- [ ] THE MINI PACKAGES: TORTELLINI
- [ ] THE RICE IMPOSTER: ORZO
- [ ] THE BLACK-TIE PASTA: BOWS
- [ ] THE POTATO PASTA: GNOCCHI
- [ ] THE WORDSMITH: ALPHABETTI SPAGHETTI
- [ ] THE FORK HOOPLA: SPAGHETTIOS

- [ ] AL DENTE
- [ ] JUST RIGHT, PLATED IMMEDIATELY
- [ ] SOGGY

- [ ] FRESH
- [ ] DRIED

+ SAUCES:
- [ ] NO SAUCE
- [ ] TOMATO
- [ ] CARBONARA
- [ ] MEAT
- [ ] PESTO
- [ ] OTHER: _____

Noodles

- [ ] THE COMMON SAVIOR: RAMEN
- [ ] THE UNCOMMON SAVIOR: UDON
- [ ] THE MINIMALIST: SOBA
- [ ] THE SHINY ONE: GLASS
- [ ] THE RICE SUBSTITUTE: RICE
- [ ] THE INSTANT GRATIFICATION: CUP

- [ ] EXTRA HARD
- [ ] HARD
- [ ] REGULAR
- [ ] SOFT
- [ ] SOGGY

- [ ] FRESH
- [ ] DRIED

+ SAUCES:
- [ ] NO SAUCE
- [ ] SWEET AND SOUR
- [ ] OYSTER
- [ ] SWEET CHILI
- [ ] BLACK BEAN
- [ ] CURRY
- [ ] MISO
- [ ] SOY
- [ ] OTHER: _____

Chilies, spice and everything nice

1. CHILIES
- [ ] LEVEL 6: DEADLY
- [ ] LEVEL 5: HELLISH
- [ ] LEVEL 4: FIRE-BREATHING
- [ ] LEVEL 3: FOR THE SWEATS
- [ ] LEVEL 2: FOR THE TASTE
- [ ] LEVEL 1: MILD, I.E., NONE

2. WASABI . . .
- [ ] YES TO THAT MAGICAL GREEN PASTE
- [ ] ITS VERY PRESENCE OFFENDS ME

. . . AND SOY SAUCE
- [ ] A NECESSITY OF LIFE
- [ ] UNNECESSARY TO LIFE

3. SALT
- [ ] IS MY FRIEND
- [ ] IS A SILENT KILLER

Soup's up

- [ ] TOMATO
- [ ] MINESTRONE
- [ ] CHICKEN
- [ ] MUSHROOM
- [ ] CHICKEN AND MUSHROOM
- [ ] SPLIT PEA
- [ ] FRENCH ONION
- [ ] MISO
- [ ] NOODLE
- [ ] BORSCHT
- [ ] GUMBO
- [ ] FISH
- [ ] OTHER: _____

AND?
- [ ] A SWIRL OF CREAM
- [ ] A SPRIG OF GARNISH
- [ ] MINI CROUTONS
- [ ] BIG CROUTONS
- [ ] NOTHING. I AM NOT A TV CHEF

OTHER COMMENTS:
_____
_____
_____

You say potato, I say fries

STATE YOUR DEEP-FRIED POTATO OF CHOICE:

- [ ] SKIN-ON FRIES
- [ ] CURLY FRIES
- [ ] THIN-CUT
- [ ] THICK-CUT
- [ ] TRIPLE-COOKED
- [ ] THE SOFT ONES
- [ ] THE LEFTOVER BITS AT THE BOTTOM OF A BOX
- [ ] WEDGES
- [ ] WAFFLE FRIES
- [ ] SWEET POTATO FRIES

FRIES GO WITH THE FOLLOWING:

- [ ] SALT
- [ ] PEPPER
- [ ] KETCHUP
- [ ] VINEGAR
- [ ] CHEESE
- [ ] CHILI
- [ ] CHILI AND CHEESE
- [ ] CHEESE CURDS AND GRAVY

- [ ] MAYONNAISE
- [ ] THOUSAND ISLAND DRESSING
- [ ] HOT SAUCE
- [ ] SATAY SAUCE
- [ ] BARBECUE SAUCE
- [ ] TARTAR SAUCE
- [ ] ONLY MORE FRIES
- [ ] OTHER:_____

May I take your order?

PLEASE STATE YOUR PREFERRED TAKE-OUT AND YOUR USUAL
ORDER FOR ULTIMATE CONVENIENCE

☐ CHINESE FROM _____
ORDER: _____

☐ PIZZA FROM _____
ORDER: _____

☐ JAPANESE / SUSHI FROM _____
ORDER: _____

☐ INDIAN / CURRY FROM _____
ORDER: _____

☐ BURGER FROM _____
ORDER: _____

☐ ITALIAN FROM _____
ORDER: _____

☐ TURKISH KEBABS FROM: _____
ORDER: _____

☐ THAI FROM _____
ORDER: _____

☐ BURRITOS FROM _____
ORDER: _____

☐ FRIED CHICKEN FROM _____
ORDER: _____

☐ OTHER: _____
ORDER: _____

OTHER INSTRUCTIONS: _____
_____
_____

29

Mind your manners

WHEN YOU DROP SOME FOOD:
- [ ] 5-SECOND RULE
- [ ] 10-SECOND RULE
- [ ] IF IT LOOKS CLEAN, IT'S PROBABLY FINE
- [ ] BLOWING ON IT WILL BANISH ANY BACTERIA
- [ ] THAT FOOD WAS DEAD TO ME AS SOON AS IT HIT THE FLOOR

WHAT SHOULD THE FOLLOWING FOODS BE EATEN WITH?

PIZZA	HANDS / KNIFE AND FORK
SUSHI	HANDS / CHOPSTICKS
BURGER	HANDS / KNIFE AND FORK
BURRITO / TACOS	HANDS / KNIFE AND FORK
CHIPS	HANDS / KNIFE AND FORK

TABLE RULES:
- [ ] NO TV
- [ ] NO DEVICES
- [ ] NO PAPERS
- [ ] DON'T SPEAK WITH YOUR MOUTH FULL
- [ ] HOLD YOUR UTENSILS PROPERLY
- [ ] SAY GRACE
- [ ] THANK THE COOK
- [ ] ASK PERMISSION TO LEAVE THE TABLE
- [ ] DON'T START EATING UNTIL EVERYONE IS SEATED

WHEN IT COMES TO FOOD:
- [ ] SHARING MAKES IT TASTE BETTER
- [ ] ALWAYS FINISH EVERYTHING—YOU NEVER KNOW WHERE YOUR NEXT MEAL IS COMING FROM
- [ ] IF IT'S IN MY VICINITY, IT'S UP FOR GRABS, EVEN IF IT'S ON YOUR PLATE
- [ ] I DON'T SHARE FOOD

OTHER RULES:

The perfect steak

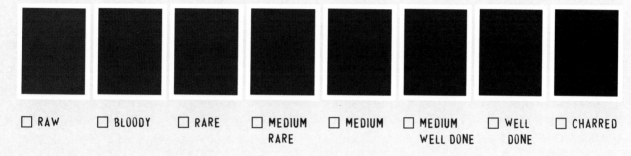

☐ RAW   ☐ BLOODY   ☐ RARE   ☐ MEDIUM RARE   ☐ MEDIUM   ☐ MEDIUM WELL DONE   ☐ WELL DONE   ☐ CHARRED

BREED OF COW /COUNTRY OF ORIGIN:_____

WITH:

PEPPERCORN SAUCE // BÉARNAISE SAUCE // MUSHROOM SAUCE // HERB BUTTER // MUSTARD // KETCHUP // GRAVY // OTHER:_____

OTHER GUIDELINES:
_____
_____

31

Let me eat cake

ALL CAKE IS GOOD, BUT NOT ALL CAKE IS CREATED EQUAL. WHAT DO YOU LIKE BEST?

TYPE:
- [ ] CHIFFON
- [ ] POUND
- [ ] FRUITCAKE
- [ ] CHEESECAKE
- [ ] RED VELVET
- [ ] SWISS ROLL
- [ ] UPSIDE DOWN
- [ ] OTHER: _____

FLAVOR:
- [ ] CHOCOLATE
- [ ] STRAWBERRY
- [ ] LEMON
- [ ] COFFEE
- [ ] CARROT
- [ ] OTHER: _____

OTHER PREFERENCES:
_____
_____

- [ ] + ICING (LOTS OF IT)
- [ ] + BUTTERCREAM (LOTS OF IT)
- [ ] + MARZIPAN (LOTS OF IT)
- [ ] + CREAM CHEESE FROSTING (LOTS OF IT)
- [ ] + MERINGUE (LOTS OF IT)

- [ ] + CHOCOLATE SAUCE
- [ ] + WHIPPED CREAM
- [ ] + ICE CREAM
- [ ] + SPRINKLES

OTHER DESSERTS:
- [ ] DONUT
- [ ] ÉCLAIR
- [ ] WAFFLE
- [ ] CUPCAKE
- [ ] MUFFIN
- [ ] BROWNIE
- [ ] COBBLER
- [ ] PIE
- [ ] TART
- [ ] COCONUT MACAROON
- [ ] FRENCH MACARON
- [ ] SOUFFLÉ
- [ ] WHOOPIE PIE
- [ ] OTHER: _____

32

The great cupcake debate...

THE ONLY CUPCAKE DEBATE THAT MATTERS

- ☐ TAKE THE "LID" (MUFFIN-TOP BIT) OFF—FROSTING, TOPPINGS AND ALL —TURN IT UPSIDE DOWN AND SMUSH IT INTO THE BASE TO MAKE AN EASY-TO-EAT CUPCAKE SANDWICH
- ☐ LICK OFF ALL THE FROSTING AND TOPPINGS, THEN SUFFER THE REST OF THE PLAIN, DRY CUPCAKE LIKE A NORMAL PERSON
- ☐ DEMOLISH CUPCAKE IN ONE MOUTHFUL

. . . .

... and the yogurt controversy

YOU KNOW WHERE YOU STAND, PICK A SIDE:

- ☐ STUFF GOES INTO YOGURT
- ☐ YOGURT GOES ONTO STUFF

NOTES: _____
_____

- ☐ MIX IT ALL UP, THEN EAT
- ☐ SCOOP A BIT OF YOGURT AND A BIT OF "STUFF" EACH TIME. REPEAT FOR EACH SPOONFUL

We all scream for ice cream

- ☐ ICE CREAM
- ☐ GELATO
- ☐ FROZEN YOGURT
- ☐ SORBET

- ☐ CHOCOLATE
- ☐ STRAWBERRY
- ☐ VANILLA
- ☐ COFFEE
- ☐ PISTACHIO
- ☐ CHOCOLATE CHIP
- ☐ RUM RAISIN
- ☐ LEMON
- ☐ RASPBERRY
- ☐ OTHER:_____

- ☐ + SPRINKLES
- ☐ + CHOCOLATE SAUCE
- ☐ + BUTTERSCOTCH
- ☐ + FRUIT
- ☐ + NUTS
- ☐ + COOKIE DOUGH
- ☐ + COOKIE PIECES
- ☐ + MOCHI
- ☐ + OTHER:_____

FLOAT?
- ☐ COLA
- ☐ GINGER ALE
- ☐ ROOT BEER
- ☐ CREAM SODA

SPECIALS
- ☐ TWO WORDS: BAKED ALASKA
- ☐ TWO MORE WORDS: KNICKERBOCKER GLORY
- ☐ TWO OTHER WORDS: BANANA SPLIT
- ☐ OTHER:_____

HOW TO SERVE:
- ☐ IN A BOWL
- ☐ IN A CONE
- ☐ A SPOON AND THE TUB

OTHER REQUESTS: _____
_____
_____

34

All the red ones belong to me

WHAT ARE YOUR FAVORITE COLOR CANDIES?

○ ○ ○ ○
○ ○ ○ ○

AND WHAT IS YOUR FAVORITE TYPE OF CANDY?

_____

OTHER DEMANDS:
_____
_____

For the love of chocolate

☐ WHITE   ☐ MILK   ☐ DARK   ☐ EXTRA DARK

☐ WITH FRUIT IN   ☐ FUDGE
☐ WITH NUTS IN   ☐ LIQUOR
☐ WITH FRUIT AND NUTS IN ☐ OTHER: _____
☐ SOFT CENTER
☐ CHILI   **PRIORITY:**
☐ ORANGE   ☐ QUALITY
☐ MINT   ☐ QUANTITY
☐ CARAMEL
☐ TOFFEE

OTHER REQUIREMENTS:
_____

Fruit bowl

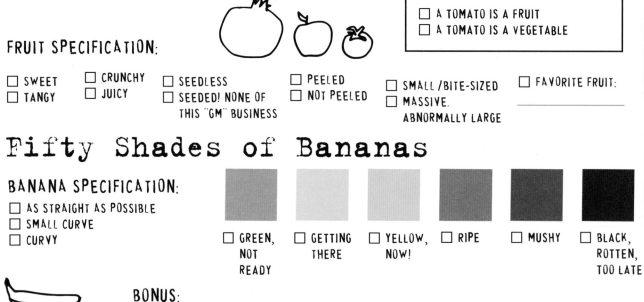

FRUIT SPECIFICATION:

- ☐ SWEET
- ☐ TANGY
- ☐ CRUNCHY
- ☐ JUICY
- ☐ SEEDLESS
- ☐ SEEDED! NONE OF THIS "GM" BUSINESS
- ☐ PEELED
- ☐ NOT PEELED
- ☐ SMALL/BITE-SIZED
- ☐ MASSIVE. ABNORMALLY LARGE
- ☐ FAVORITE FRUIT: _____

RE: Tomatoes
- ☐ A TOMATO IS A FRUIT
- ☐ A TOMATO IS A VEGETABLE

Fifty Shades of Bananas

BANANA SPECIFICATION:

- ☐ AS STRAIGHT AS POSSIBLE
- ☐ SMALL CURVE
- ☐ CURVY

- ☐ GREEN, NOT READY
- ☐ GETTING THERE
- ☐ YELLOW, NOW!
- ☐ RIPE
- ☐ MUSHY
- ☐ BLACK, ROTTEN, TOO LATE

BONUS:
- ☐ BLEMISH FREE
- ☐ WITH A FEW SPOTS
- ☐ WITH SPOTS ALL OVER

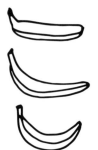

OTHER NOTES:
_____
_____
_____

Snack house

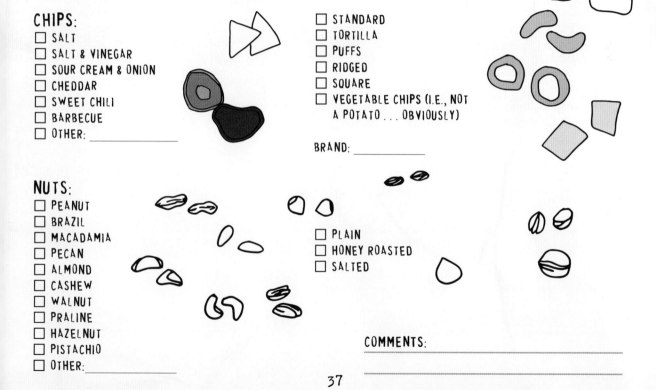

CHIPS:
- ☐ SALT
- ☐ SALT & VINEGAR
- ☐ SOUR CREAM & ONION
- ☐ CHEDDAR
- ☐ SWEET CHILI
- ☐ BARBECUE
- ☐ OTHER: _____

- ☐ STANDARD
- ☐ TORTILLA
- ☐ PUFFS
- ☐ RIDGED
- ☐ SQUARE
- ☐ VEGETABLE CHIPS (I.E., NOT A POTATO ... OBVIOUSLY)

BRAND: _____

NUTS:
- ☐ PEANUT
- ☐ BRAZIL
- ☐ MACADAMIA
- ☐ PECAN
- ☐ ALMOND
- ☐ CASHEW
- ☐ WALNUT
- ☐ PRALINE
- ☐ HAZELNUT
- ☐ PISTACHIO
- ☐ OTHER: _____

- ☐ PLAIN
- ☐ HONEY ROASTED
- ☐ SALTED

COMMENTS: _____

37

All washed up

WHAT IS YOUR POLICY ON DEALING WITH DIRTY DISHES?

☐ DID YOU JUST USE IT? WASH IT! WASH IT NOW!
   THERE'S A SPECIAL CIRCLE OF HELL RESERVED FOR THOSE
   WHO LEAVE THEIR DISHES FOR OTHER PEOPLE TO DO
☐ "I'LL DO IT LATER" (THIS IS TRUE)
☐ "I'LL DO IT LATER" (THIS IS NOT TRUE)
☐ "I WILL USE EVERY LAST ITEM IN THE KITCHEN AND PERHAPS
   EVEN BUY NEW ITEMS UNTIL EVERYTHING CONCEIVABLY
   USABLE IS DIRTY. THEN I WILL CONSIDER WASHING THEM"
☐ I HAVE A CLEANER FOR THAT

WHAT IS YOUR POLICY ON LEAVING DIRTY DISHES AROUND
THE HOUSE (NOT EVEN STACKED BY THE SINK)?

☐ THE JOURNEY TO THE KITCHEN IS OFTEN TOO MUCH. IT IS ACCEPTABLE, NAY, SENSIBLE TO LEAVE ITEMS
   LYING AROUND AND DO THEM ALL AT ONCE LATER
☐ THE VERY PRACTICE IS REPULSIVE. I FROWN CONDESCENDINGLY UPON IT
☐ TOTALLY UNACCEPTABLE. IT WILL ATTRACT RATS AND THINGS

OTHER JUDGMENTS: _____
_____

A house divided

HERE ARE TWO BIG ONES. ARE YOU READY?
DEFEND YOUR CORNER ON DOING THE DISHES

HOW TO DO THE DISHES:

- [ ] WASH THEM ALL IN ONE BOWL. SAVE WATER. SAVE MONEY. SAVE THE WORLD
- [ ] LEAVE THE FAUCET RUNNING AND RINSE ALL ITEMS SEPARATELY. OTHERWISE IT'S NOT CLEANING, IT'S "GREASING" — A WASTE OF TIME, A WASTE OF RESOURCES

HOW TO LOAD THE DISHWASHER PROPERLY (OH DEAR . . .)

- [ ] CUTLERY UP (SO IT DOESN'T GET BLUNT)
- [ ] CUTLERY DOWN (SO NO ONE GETS STABBED)

- [ ] BOWLS AND PLATES TILTED DOWN
- [ ] BOWLS AND PLATES STOOD UP SIDEWAYS

- [ ] NOT TOO FULL, OTHERWISE NOTHING GETS PROPERLY CLEAN
- [ ] NO METHOD, AS LONG AS THE DISHWASHER IS FILLED TO MAXIMUM CAPACITY. IT'S LIKE SOLVING ONE OF THOSE CHINESE LOGIC PUZZLES

- [ ] WE DON'T HAVE A DISHWASHER

OTHER REMARKS:
_____
_____

CHAPTER 2: BATHROOM

Scrubbing up

WHICH DO YOU PREFER?
- ☐ SHOWER
- ☐ BATH
- ☐ SINK AND WASHCLOTH
- ☐ NONE OF THE ABOVE

TIME OF DAY?
- ☐ MORNING: _____ A.M., BEFORE GOING OUT
- ☐ NIGHT: _____ P.M., BEFORE BED
- ☐ BOTH
- ☐ AND ALSO AFTER SPORTS/EXERCISE

OTHER PREFERENCES:
_____
_____
_____
_____

Squeaky clean

JUST HOW LONG DOES IT TAKE YOU TO FEEL CLEAN, OR DO YOU PRIDE YOURSELF
ON HOW QUICKLY YOU CAN GET IN AND OUT OF THE BATHROOM?

TO TAKE A SHOWER / HAVE A BATH, YOU NEED:

- [ ] < 1 MINUTE
- [ ] 1–5 MINUTES
- [ ] 5–10 MINUTES
- [ ] 10–20 MINUTES
- [ ] 30–60 MINUTES
- [ ] 1 HOUR +

BRUSHING TEETH

HOW OFTEN? _____

WHEN? _____

HOW LONG FOR? _____

AND HOW OFTEN DO YOU NEED TO WASH TO FEEL HUMAN?

- [ ] MORE THAN ONCE A DAY
- [ ] EVERY DAY
- [ ] A FEW TIMES A WEEK
- [ ] EVERY NOW AND THEN
- [ ] WHEN I START TO SMELL
- [ ] NOT EVEN THEN

NOTES: _____

_____

_____

The perfect soak

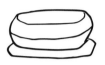

PREFERRED HOTNESS:
- ☐ COLD
- ☐ MILD
- ☐ HOT
- ☐ BOIL A LOBSTER

EXTRAS:
- ☐ + SOAP
- ☐ + FANCY SCENTED SOAP
- ☐ + BUBBLE BATH. BRAND: _____
- ☐ + VERY SPECIFIC SHOWER GEL. BRAND: _____
- ☐ + BATH SALTS
- ☐ + FOAM
- ☐ + EXFOLIANT SCRUB
- ☐ + BABY OIL
- ☐ + SHAMPOO. BRAND: _____
- ☐ + CONDITIONER. BRAND: _____
- ☐ + SHAMPOO AND CONDITIONER 2-IN-1 MULTI-TASKER. BRAND: _____
- ☐ + ONE OF THOSE SHAMPOO, CONDITIONER, BODY WASH ALL-IN-ONE MAGICAL INVENTIONS. BRAND: _____
- ☐ NONE OF THE ABOVE, JUST THE WATER, THANKS

OTHER CONDITIONS
_____
_____

Bath-Bathrooms are...

MARK ALL THAT APPLY:

☐ FOR SINGING IN! (GREAT ACOUSTICS)
☐ NOT FOR SINGING IN (DESPITE THE GREAT ACOUSTICS)
☐ FOR READING IN
☐ FOR PLAYING VIDEO GAMES IN
☐ FOR BROWSING THE INTERNET IN
☐ FOR LIGHTING CANDLES AND RELAXING IN
☐ FOR GETTING CLEAN IN. END OF STORY

OTHER COMMENTS:

_____
_____
_____
_____

Serious business:
Towel type and color

A TOWEL SHOULD BE:
- [ ] COLD
- [ ] WARM AND TOASTY

- [ ] SMALL
- [ ] MEDIUM
- [ ] LARGE
- [ ] PROPERLY WRAP-AROUND LARGE, LIKE A SHEET

- [ ] WAFFLE
- [ ] TERRY
- [ ] TUMBLE-DRIED—THE ONLY WAY TO ACHIEVE THE ACCEPTABLE LEVEL OF FLUFFINESS

- [ ] WHITE
- [ ] CREAM
- [ ] BLUE
- [ ] GREEN
- [ ] RED
- [ ] PURPLE
- [ ] PINK
- [ ] YELLOW
- [ ] BROWN
- [ ] GRAY
- [ ] BLACK
- [ ] PATTERNED/MOTIF:_____

LEVEL OF MAINTENANCE
- [ ] CLEAN. I.E., WASHED AFTER EVERY USE
- [ ] CLEAN. I.E., NOT DIRTY. WHY WASH IT? IT'S A TOWEL! FOR AFTER YOU'VE CLEANED YOURSELF!

WHERE TOWELS LIVE AFTER USE:
- [ ] FLOOR
- [ ] RADIATOR
- [ ] TOWEL RAIL
- [ ] CHAIR
- [ ] CLOSET

- [ ] I PREFER TO AIR-DRY

OTHER NOTES:
_____
_____
_____

44

Places to go, people to see

HOW LONG DOES IT TAKE YOU TO GET READY?

IN THE MORNING:
- ☐ < 5 MINUTES
- ☐ 5–10 MINUTES
- ☐ 10–20 MINUTES
- ☐ 20–30 MINUTES
- ☐ 30–60 MINUTES
- ☐ 1+ HOURS: ____ HOURS

FOR AN EVENT:
- ☐ < 5 MINUTES
- ☐ 5–10 MINUTES
- ☐ 10–20 MINUTES
- ☐ 20–30 MINUTES
- ☐ 30–60 MINUTES
- ☐ 1+ HOURS: ____ HOURS

OTHER ARRANGEMENTS:
_____
_____
_____

The toilet seat situation

☐ UP
☐ DOWN
☐ I REALLY DON'T CARE. IT DOESN'T KILL ME TO LIFT OR LOWER A SEAT.
    BUT SO HELP ME, YOU WILL AIM PROPERLY *

*HOW OFTEN SHOULD THE TOILET BE CLEANED? _____

... AND WHO SHOULD CLEAN IT?
☐ THE PERSON WHO USED IT
☐ EVERYONE
☐ NAME: _____

HOW OFTEN SHOULD YOU FLUSH?
☐ AFTER EVERY USE, OBVIOUSLY!
☐ NOT NECESSARY AFTER NUMBER ONES
☐ WHEN I CAN BE BOTHERED

OTHER NOTES: _____
_____

The toilet paper saga

☐ FACING IN ☐ FACING OUT * ☐ WITH THE POINTY TAB, LIKE IN HOTELS

* NOTE: IF YOU WERE EVER IN ANY DOUBT AS TO WHICH IS THE RIGHT CHOICE, HAVE YOU NOTICED THAT HOTELS ALWAYS LEAVE THE ROLL FACING OUT, WITH THE TAB ON THE OUTSIDE? ENOUGH SAID

COMMENTS: _____

Toilet paper diplomacy

- ☐ IF YOU START THE SECOND-TO-LAST ROLL OF TOILET PAPER, IT'S YOUR TURN TO GET MORE
- ☐ IF YOU START THE LAST ROLL OF TOILET PAPER, IT'S YOUR TURN TO GET MORE
- ☐ WHOEVER'S DOING THE SHOPPING—MAKE SURE WE HAVE ENOUGH GENERALLY*

- ☐ IF YOU USE THE LAST PIECE, YOU WILL THROW AWAY THE TUBE AND PUT A NEW ROLL IN PLACE. THIS IS NOT OPTIONAL. CHECK OFF THIS BOX. CHECK IT

*IF YOU SEE IT ON SALE, STOCK UP. THERE'S A SPECIAL PLACE FOR YOU IN HEAVEN

Toilet paper specification

COLOR: _____

PATTERN: _____

PREFERRED BRAND: _____

- ☐ 1-PLY
- ☐ 2-PLY
- ☐ 3-PLY
- ☐ 4-PLY?

- ☐ QUILTED
- ☐ EXTRA SOFT
- ☐ RECYCLED
- ☐ WHATEVER'S CHEAPEST, IT'S TOILET PAPER

- ☐ BIDET

OTHER DEMANDS:

_____

_____

_____

48

Toilet-Bathrooms are...

(PLEASE CHECK OFF ALL THAT APPLY)

- ☐ FOR PLAYING VIDEO GAMES IN
- ☐ FOR PHONING / MESSAGING IN
- ☐ FOR READING IN
- ☐ FOR BROWSING THE INTERNET IN
- ☐ THE ONLY PLACE WHERE I CAN GET SOME PEACE / PRIVACY
- ☐ TOILETS. DON'T HANG AROUND. GET IN, GET OUT, MOVE ON!

☐ DO NOT DISTURB WHEN ON THE TOILET! BUT HOW LONG IS IT ACCEPTABLE TO STAY IN THERE? _____

Toilet-Bathroom decor

MARK ALL THAT ARE ACCEPTABLE. CROSS OUT ANY THAT ARE UNACCEPTABLE

- ☐ AWARDS I HAVE WON
- ☐ AWARDS MY CHILDREN HAVE WON
- ☐ WORKS OF LITERATURE
- ☐ MAGAZINES / NEWSPAPERS
- ☐ JOKE BOOKS
- ☐ RANDOM STOCK PHOTOGRAPHY / ARTWORK
- ☐ POTPOURRI
- ☐ AIR FRESHENER
- ☐ CANDLE
- ☐ TELEVISION

NOTES:
_____
_____
_____

49

CHAPTER 3: LIVING ROOM

How do you organize your stuff?

☐ ALPHABETICALLY AND BY SUBJECT
☐ CHRONOLOGICALLY / BY DATE
☐ BY COLOR
☐ OTHER SYSTEM:_____
☐ WHAT DO YOU MEAN, "ORGANIZE"?

WALLS ARE FOR:
☐ ART
☐ POSTERS
☐ DISHES
☐ MIRRORS
☐ SHELVES
☐ DARTBOARDS

☐ STUFFED ANIMAL HEADS
☐ PHOTOGRAPHS
☐ WALLPAPER
☐ OTHER: _____

How much stuff do you have?

☐ COULD GIVE A DRAGON A RUN FOR ITS MONEY
☐ COULD GIVE A SQUIRREL A RUN FOR ITS MONEY
☐ COULD ALMOST BE ON A TV SHOW ABOUT HOARDING
☐ COULD OPEN A THRIFT STORE
☐ SENTIMENTALIST (MOST ITEMS ARE MEANINGFUL)
☐ AESTHETICIST (MINIMAL, WELL-CURATED SELECTION, LIKE IN ONE OF THOSE WHITE-WALLED ART GALLERIES)
☐ UTILITARIAN (ONLY ITEMS THAT HAVE A PURPOSE)
☐ SPARTAN (ONLY WHAT'S ABSOLUTELY NECESSARY)

AND WHAT'S THE POLICY ON PERSONAL POSSESSIONS?

☐ WHAT'S MINE IS MINE
☐ WHAT'S YOURS IS YOURS
☐ MINE IS OURS
☐ WHAT DO YOU MEAN I CAN'T USE YOUR STUFF?!

What's on the (coffee) table?

- ☐ COFFEE TABLE BOOKS, FOR SHOW
- ☐ COFFEE TABLE BOOKS, AS COASTERS
- ☐ MAGAZINES AND NEWSPAPERS
- ☐ MAGAZINES AND NEWSPAPERS, AS COASTERS
- ☐ ACTUAL COASTERS

- ☐ CHESS SET, FOR SHOW
- ☐ CHESS SET, FOR PLAY
- ☐ NOTHING
- ☐ IT'S A FOOTREST, REALLY

Who's been sitting in my chair?

WHERE DO YOU LIKE TO SIT?

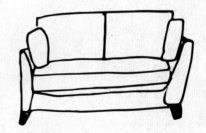

- ☐ LEFT-SIDE OF THE SOFA
- ☐ MIDDLE
- ☐ RIGHT-SIDE OF THE SOFA
- ☐ DRAPED OVER MY OWN ARMCHAIR, THANKS

- ☐ BEANBAG
- ☐ BIG FLOOR CUSHIONS
- ☐ JUST ON THE FLOOR

AND WHAT IS YOUR POLICY ON CUSHIONS?

- ☐ SCATTERED
- ☐ NEAT
- ☐ "COMFORTABLE" (A MESS)

OTHER NOTES: _____
_____
_____

Do not disturb when I am:

- [ ] GAMING
- [ ] DOING YOGA, PILATES, OR MEDITATING
- [ ] WORKING
- [ ] ASLEEP
- [ ] READING
- [ ] TAKING A CALL
- [ ] OTHER: _____

OTHER THINGS TO REMEMBER:
_____
_____
_____
_____

House music
ARE YOU OLD SCHOOL, NEW SCHOOL,
OR ACTUALLY JUST A HIPSTER?

FAVORITE MEDIUM:
- ☐ STREAM
- ☐ CD
- ☐ TAPE
- ☐ VINYL
- ☐ RADIO
- ☐ INSTRUMENT /LIVE

ARTISTS /GENRES THAT
I REFUSE TO LISTEN TO:

_____
_____
_____
_____

☐ ^ IF YOU INSIST ON
HAVING SUCH POOR TASTE
IN MUSIC, PLEASE LISTEN
VIA HEADPHONES

Computer love
- ☐ TEAM MAC
- ☐ TEAM PC

FAVORITE PIECE OF TECH?
- ☐ PHONE
- ☐ TABLET
- ☐ PHABLET
- ☐ LAPTOP
- ☐ DESKTOP
- ☐ TYPEWRITER
- ☐ PEN AND PAPER

NOTES ON DOWNLOADING:
- ☐ DON'T RESTART THE WI-FI WITHOUT GIVING ME
NOTICE FIRST
- ☐ DON'T USE THE WI-FI TO DOWNLOAD CRAPPY TV OR
QUESTIONABLE VIDEOS—IT SLOWS THINGS DOWN AND
I'LL HATE YOU AND THE WORLD, BUT MOSTLY YOU

OTHER COMMENTS:
_____
_____

Rules of the remote control

HOW TO SETTLE DISAGREEMENTS OVER WHO GETS TO DECIDE WHAT TO WATCH OR PLAY ON THE BOX

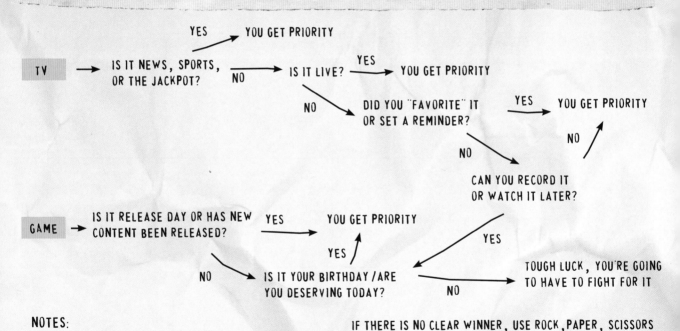

TV → IS IT NEWS, SPORTS, OR THE JACKPOT?

- YES → YOU GET PRIORITY
- NO → IS IT LIVE?
  - YES → YOU GET PRIORITY
  - NO → DID YOU "FAVORITE" IT OR SET A REMINDER?
    - YES → YOU GET PRIORITY
    - NO → CAN YOU RECORD IT OR WATCH IT LATER?
      - YES → YOU GET PRIORITY
      - NO → (see below)

GAME — IS IT RELEASE DAY OR HAS NEW CONTENT BEEN RELEASED?

- YES → YOU GET PRIORITY
- NO → IS IT YOUR BIRTHDAY / ARE YOU DESERVING TODAY?
  - YES → YOU GET PRIORITY
  - NO → TOUGH LUCK, YOU'RE GOING TO HAVE TO FIGHT FOR IT

NOTES: _____

IF THERE IS NO CLEAR WINNER, USE ROCK, PAPER, SCISSORS OR A DUEL TO COME TO A DECISION. GOOD LUCK

Regular scheduled programming will now resume

HOW SHOULD TV / FILMS BE WATCHED?

- ☐ ON THE TELEVISION
- ☐ ON A TABLET, COMPUTER, OR SMARTPHONE
- ☐ IN THE HOME CINEMA, OF COURSE
- ☐ VIA THE PROJECTOR FOR THE PROPER EFFECT

- ☐ BY MYSELF
- ☐ WITH OTHERS, THE MORE THE BETTER

WHEN YOU'VE AGREED TO WATCH WITH ME:

- ☐ WAIT UNTIL WE CAN WATCH IT TOGETHER
- ☐ IF YOU WATCH SOMETHING WITHOUT ME THAT WE'VE BEEN SAVING TO WATCH TOGETHER, AT LEAST HAVE THE DECENCY TO FAKE LAUGH AND CRY AT THE RIGHT MOMENTS, AS IF WATCHING FOR THE FIRST TIME
- ☐ IF YOU WATCH WITHOUT ME, I WILL NEVER FORGIVE YOU

THE FOLLOWING MUST ALWAYS BE SHOWN THE UTMOST RESPECT:

FILMS:

_____

_____

TV PROGRAMS:

_____

_____

ACTORS / ACTRESSES / CELEBRITIES:

_____

_____

BONUS RULE

- ☐ IF YOU DELETE MY SAVED PROGRAM, THE TELEVISION DEMON WILL SMITE YOU DOWN AND EVERYONE WILL AGREE THAT HE WAS RIGHT TO DO SO

OTHER RULES:

_____

_____

_____

When watching TV or a film, talking is...

- ☐ WELCOMED
- ☐ TOLERATED
- ☐ PUNISHABLE BY DEATH

THE FOLLOWING ARE NOT ALLOWED:

- ☐ EATING
- ☐ VACUUMING
- ☐ MAKING CALLS
- ☐ MAKING OUT

OTHER NOTES:
_____
_____
_____

Where's the remote?!

☐ PLEASE DRAW AN "X" ON THE SPOT THE REMOTE CONTROL SHOULD BE RETURNED TO SO THAT YOU ALWAYS KNOW WHERE IT IS. ALTERNATIVELY, IF THERE IS NO SUCH LOCATION OR IF YOU ENJOY PLAYING "HUNT THE REMOTE," MARK ALL THE PLACES IT COULD POSSIBLY BE WITH A "?."

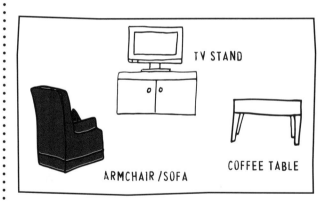

TV STAND

ARMCHAIR / SOFA

COFFEE TABLE

OTHER INSTRUCTIONS:
_____
_____

On borrowing books from me

HOW SHOULD BOOKS BE RETURNED TO YOU?

☐ PREFERABLY IN MINT CONDITION. I WANT TO SEE NO SIGNS THAT IT HAS BEEN TOUCHED BY HUMAN HANDS *

☐ MILD WEAR AND TEAR IS O.K., BOOKS ARE MEANT TO BE LOVED BUT RESPECTED. I PROBABLY WON'T EVER READ IT AGAIN ANYWAY

☐ IT'S A BOOK. TAKE IT INTO THE BATH, TO THE BEACH, LEAVE IT WITH A SMALL CHILD OR A PET, IT'S FINE. AS LONG AS YOU ENJOYED READING IT

NOTES ON FINES, RETURN DATES, OTHER:

WHOEVER DOESN'T RETURN A BOOK:

☐ IS WELCOME TO IT. I'M DROWNING IN THEM

☐ IS DEAD TO ME. I'LL PRETEND IT DOESN'T MATTER, MAYBE CASUALLY ASKING AFTER THE BOOK NOW AND THEN OR PERHAPS NOT MENTIONING IT AT ALL, WHEN, IN FACT, I WILL PLOT MY REVENGE EVERY DAY UNTIL ITS SAFE RETURN

RE: eBooks

☐ THEY'RE GREAT
☐ THEY'RE O.K.
☐ SACRILEGE

* No dog ears, no cracked spines, no annotations. We're talking library rules, and not your local library where people tear out pages and leave suspicious stains. No, the ones where they search you when you go in and again when you leave. I should be able to return that book to a bookstore and no one would ever know it had been read.

CHAPTER 4: BEDROOM

Wakey wakey...

STATE YOUR SLEEP PATTERNS SO OTHERS KNOW WHEN NOT TO DISTURB YOU

I USUALLY GET UP...

- ☐ AT _____ A.M.
- ☐ AT _____ P.M.
- ☐ AT DAWN
- ☐ AT A REASONABLE HOUR
- ☐ AFTER NOON

AT WEEKENDS OR ON DAYS OFF, I USUALLY GET UP...

- ☐ AT _____ A.M.
- ☐ AT _____ P.M.
- ☐ AT DAWN (STUPID BODY CLOCK!)
- ☐ AT A REASONABLE HOUR
- ☐ AFTER NOON
- ☐ WHAT'S A DAY OFF?

NEVER, EVER WAKE ME BEFORE:

- ☐ _____ A.M.
- ☐ _____ P.M.
- ☐ DAWN
- ☐ A REASONABLE HOUR
- ☐ NOON

I AM A:

- ☐ LARK /MORNING PERSON
- ☐ NIGHT OWL /VAMPIRE

OTHER WARNINGS:

_____
_____
_____

Night night, sleep tight

WHEN DO YOU USUALLY GO TO BED? PLEASE MARK THE TIME ON THE CLOCK FACE

☐ A.M.

☐ P.M.

☐ LIGHTS OUT
☐ "LIGHTS OUT" BUT ACTUALLY LIGHTS STAY ON—SCARED OF THE DARK / WARY OF BURGLARS AND ASSASSINS

OTHER NOTES:
_____
_____
_____

Don't let the bedbugs bite

BED SPECIFICATION:

☐ SINGLE
☐ DOUBLE
☐ QUEEN
☐ KING
☐ EMPEROR
☐ ROUND

☐ BUNK BED /LOFT
☐ FOUR-POSTER
☐ HAMMOCK
☐ WATERBED
☐ FUTON
☐ OTHER: _____

☐ HARD
☐ BOUNCY
☐ SOFT

BEDDING SPECIFICATION:

☐ SHEETS AND BLANKETS
☐ DOWN COMFORTER/QUILT

☐ PLAIN
☐ COLOR: _____
☐ PATTERNED: _____
☐ OTHER: _____

Pillow talk

WHAT ARE YOUR PILLOW PREFERENCES?

☐ HARD
☐ SOFT
☐ FLUFFY
☐ DOWN
☐ HYPOALLERGENIC
☐ SCENTED
☐ OTHER: _____

HOW MANY PILLOWS DO YOU NEED?

☐ ONE, LIKE A NORMAL PERSON
☐ TWO, LIKE AN INDULGENT PERSON
☐ THREE, LIKE AN EXTRAVAGANT PERSON
☐ FOUR+ BECAUSE IT FEELS LIKE A CLOUD, O.K?

OTHER DEMANDS: _____

Sweet dreams are made of this

WHAT DO YOU NEED FOR THE PERFECT SLEEP ENVIRONMENT?

LIGHT
- ☐ LIGHTS ON, DIMMED
- ☐ LIGHTS ON IN THE HALLWAY
- ☐ LIGHTS OFF
- ☐ LIGHTS OFF, BLACKOUT CURTAINS, AND AN EYEMASK

TEMPERATURE
- ☐ WARM, SNUG AS A BUG
- ☐ COOL, WINDOW OPEN

SOUND
- ☐ QUIET / SILENCE
- ☐ EARPLUGS NEEDED, TOTAL SILENCE
- ☐ LITTLE BIT OF WHITE NOISE
- ☐ WHALE SONG NEEDED
- ☐ RADIO NEEDED
- ☐ SPORTS RESULTS NEEDED
- ☐ OTHER: _____

MY BEDTIME ROUTINE IS:
_____
_____
_____

THE LUCKY ONES
- ☐ YEAH, I CAN SLEEP ANYTIME, ANYWHERE

OTHER NOTES:
_____
_____
_____
_____

61

Insomniacs and somnambulists

THINGS YOU SHOULD KNOW ABOUT MY SLEEPING HABITS

PLEASE BEAR IN MIND THAT I:

☐ SLEEPWALK
☐ KICK OFF THE COVERS
☐ FIGHT WITH ENEMIES (I.E. BEDCOVERS OR ANYONE NEARBY)
   WHEN DREAMING
☐ CAN SLEEP WITH MY EYES OPEN

☐ MUTTER IN MY SLEEP
☐ SNORE (NOT THAT BADLY)
☐ SNORE (BADLY)
☐ SNORE (MEASURES-ON-THE-RICHTER-SCALE BADLY)

☐ HAVE INSOMNIA
☐ AM THE LIGHTEST OF SLEEPERS
☐ COULD SLEEP THROUGH THE APOCALYPSE

OTHER NOTICES:
_____
_____

Primary use of the bedroom

☐ WORK
☐ REST
☐ PLAY

HOW IMPORTANT IS SLEEP TO YOU?

☐ SLEEP IS BASICALLY MY FAVORITE THING. IDEALLY I NEED _____ HOURS OF SLEEP.
  AND WILL COMPLAIN AND TELL EVERYONE I KNOW IF I GET ANYTHING LESS
☐ YOU CAN SLEEP WHEN YOU'RE DEAD

OTHER THOUGHTS: _____

_____

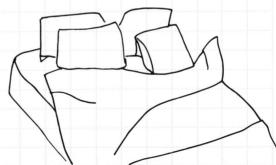

CHAPTER 5: YARD

The great outdoors

WHAT SHOULD YOUR OUTDOOR SPACE BE USED FOR?
MARK ON THE CHART AND ADD YOUR OWN ACTIVITIES

☐ DON'T HAVE ONE

AESTHETICAL / FOR LOOKS (vertical axis)

RECREATIONAL / FOR FUN (horizontal axis)

☐ CORN MAZE

☐ NOTHING. IT'S THERE
TO LOOK IMMACULATE.
DON'T WALK ON THE
GRASS. NO BALL GAMES

☐ GOLF

☐ CROQUET

☐ GROWING FLOWERS

☐ PICNICS /PARTIES /
BARBECUES

☐ FOOTBALL

☐ RELAXING

☐ BADMINTON

☐ EXTREME
SPORTS

☐ FRESH AIR

☐ GROWING FOOD

☐ FRISBEE

☐ SOMEWHERE TO HANG
OUT THE LAUNDRY

☐ KEEPING ANIMALS

☐ DIY PROJECTS

☐ SCIENCE
EXPERIMENTS

☐ SMOKING

Lawn specification

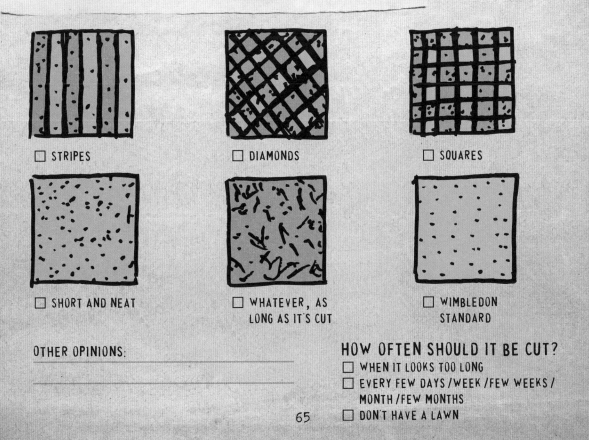

☐ STRIPES

☐ DIAMONDS

☐ SQUARES

☐ SHORT AND NEAT

☐ WHATEVER, AS LONG AS IT'S CUT

☐ WIMBLEDON STANDARD

OTHER OPINIONS: _____

_____

HOW OFTEN SHOULD IT BE CUT?
☐ WHEN IT LOOKS TOO LONG
☐ EVERY FEW DAYS/WEEK/FEW WEEKS/ MONTH/FEW MONTHS
☐ DON'T HAVE A LAWN

Gardening chores

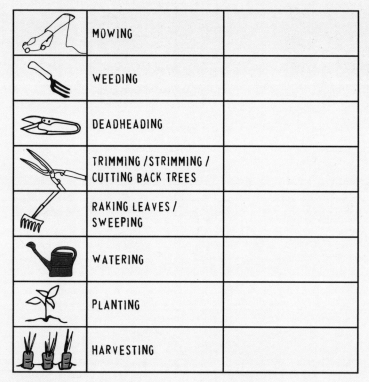

	MOWING	
	WEEDING	
	DEADHEADING	
	TRIMMING / STRIMMING / CUTTING BACK TREES	
	RAKING LEAVES / SWEEPING	
	WATERING	
	PLANTING	
	HARVESTING	

WHETHER YOU CONSIDER IT WORK OR PLEASURE, YARD WORK NEEDS TO BE DONE! WHO DOES WHAT?

OTHER NOTES:

_____

_____

_____

_____

Ranger duties

		SIGN UP / DELEGATE HERE:
	SCARING OFF FOXES, WOLVES, BEARS, MOUNTAIN LIONS, ETC.	
	KEEPING LESS DANGEROUS WILDLIFE / ANIMALS FED AND WATERED, E.G., BIRDS, SQUIRRELS, BUTTERFLIES	
	GETTING RID OF SLUGS AND SNAILS—BAG THEM	
	ANT, BUG, AND OTHER PEST CONTROL	
	MAKING SURE THE PROPERTY IS WELL FORTIFIED— MAINTAINING GATES, FENCES, WALLS	
	SHOVELLING SNOW OFF THE SIDEWALK / DRIVEWAY AND THROWING SALT AND / OR GRIT	
	CLEANING THE POND, IF THERE IS ONE	
	CLEANING CARS / VEHICLES, IF ANY	

67

Absolute power

LIGHTS:
- ☐ ALWAYS TURN THE LIGHTS OFF WHEN YOU LEAVE THE ROOM! GHOSTS DON'T NEED LIGHT
- ☐ I COULD NOT CARE LESS IF PEOPLE LEAVE THE LIGHTS ON
- ☐ I ONLY CARE BECAUSE OF THE ELECTRICITY BILL. TURN LIGHTS OFF AS MUCH AS POSSIBLE

TOO COLD?
- ☐ TURN THE HEATING UP
- ☐ PUT ON A SWEATER
- ☐ RUN AROUND TO GET WARM

TOO HOT?
- ☐ TURN ON THE FAN / AIR CONDITIONING
- ☐ OPEN A WINDOW
- ☐ EAT SOME ICE CREAM

OTHER COMMANDS:
_____
_____
_____
_____

PLUGS, SOCKETS AND APPLIANCES:
- ☐ ALWAYS TURN APPLIANCES OFF WHEN NOT IN USE. THEY ARE CRYING INSIDE FROM OVERWORK AND WE WILL ALL DIE IN A FIRE
- ☐ ALRIGHT, ALWAYS TURN STUFF OFF WHEN NOT IN USE, BUT ONLY BECAUSE OF THE BILL AGAIN
- ☐ SAVE THE PLANET! TURN STUFF OFF. STANDBY MODE IS NOT GOOD ENOUGH
- ☐ I BELIEVE SCIENTISTS WILL FIGURE OUT HOW TO SOLVE THE ENERGY PROBLEM, SO I'M NOT THAT BOTHERED ABOUT TURNING STUFF OFF
- ☐ WE HAVE OUR OWN SOLAR PANELS / GREEN ENERGY. WE DO WHAT WE LIKE

Preferred state of room

PLEASE PUT AN "X" ON THE DIAGRAM TO SHOW YOUR PREFERENCE

MINIMALIST

JAPANESE

SCANDINAVIAN

ZEN-LIKE

ORGANIZED
CHAOS

ACTUALLY JUST
CHAOS

Chores list

	COOKING	
	DISHES	
	LAUNDRY	
	IRONING	
	VACUUMING	
	CLEANING	
	TIDYING	
	OTHER	

FIVE HOUSEHOLD CHORES **I DON'T DO** AND NEVER WILL, NOT FOR ANYBODY

1) ....

2) ....

3) ....

4) ....

5) ....

Weekly essentials

WEEK 1:	
WEEK 2:	
WEEK 3:	
WEEK 4:	

PLEASE FILL IN THE ROTA OR SELECT ONE OF THE FOLLOWING TO SHOW WHO SHOULD DO THE SHOPPING:
DESIGNATED SHOPPING PERSON:
_____

☐ EVERYONE GETS WHAT THEY WANT, WHENEVER

WHERE SHOULD FOOD BE BOUGHT FROM PREFERABLY?
☐ SUPERMARKET. NAME:_____
☐ ONLINE. FROM: _____
☐ FARMER'S MARKET
☐ LOCAL STORES
☐ OTHER: _____

SHOPPING LIST
ALWAYS CHECK THAT
WE HAVE ENOUGH:

☐ MILK
☐ TOILET PAPER
☐ COFFEE
☐ BREAD
☐ EGGS
☐ SUGAR
☐ _____
☐ _____
☐ _____
☐ _____
☐ _____

The shopping bag saga

HOW TO DEAL WITH PAPER /PLASTIC BAGS

☐ KEEP AND REUSE
☐ THROW AWAY! WHAT WOULD YOU KEEP THEM FOR?
☐ I HAVE A REUSABLE BAG AND I WILL USE IT FOR THE REST OF MY LIFE

OTHER NOTES:
_____
_____
_____
_____

71

Trash and drains

WHAT IS YOUR POLICY ON TRASH AND RECYCLING?

- ☐ DUTIFULLY FOLLOW THE COLOR CODED TRASH CAN POLICY
- ☐ TRASH CAN COLORS ARE MORE LIKE GUIDELINES
- ☐ GLOBAL WARMING ISN'T EVEN A REAL THING

WHO SHOULD EMPTY THE TRASH IN THE HOUSE?

_____

WHO SHOULD REPLACE THE BAGS?

_____

WHAT DAY SHOULD THE TRASH GO OUT?

_____

WHO SHOULD TAKE THE TRASH OUT?

_____

WHAT IS YOUR POLICY ON UNBLOCKING DRAINS AND GUTTERS?

- ☐ WHOEVER BLOCKED IT SHOULD UNBLOCK IT
- ☐ IF EVERYONE JUST CLEANED UP THEIR OWN HAIR AND BITS OF FOOD FROM THE SINK, LIFE WOULD BE SO MUCH EASIER
- ☐ DESIGNATED PERSON _____ WILL UNBLOCK IT

IN TERMS OF RECYCLING:

- ☐ I AM AN ECO-WARRIOR
- ☐ I MAKE A TOKEN EFFORT
- ☐ I COULD NOT CARE LESS

OTHER OPINIONS:

_____

_____

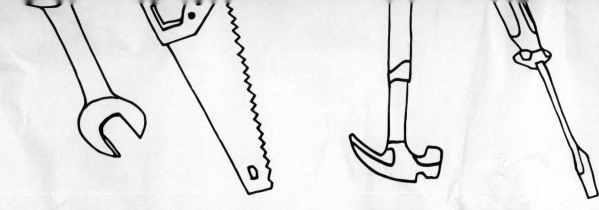

When it comes to mending/ fixing things...

☐ PAY SOMEONE TO DO IT, EVEN IF IT'S CHANGING A LIGHTBULB
☐ FOR EASY STUFF LIKE SETTING UP WI-FI OR REPLACING A FUSE,
  WE'RE FINE—BUT NEED TO CALL IN A PROFESSIONAL FOR
  MOST OTHER THINGS
☐ PAY SOMEONE TO FIX IT ONLY IF NECESSARY. WE'RE TALKING
  BROKEN FURNACE, HOLE IN THE ROOF, OR RAT INFESTATION.
  OTHERWISE I WILL DO IT WHETHER QUALIFIED OR NOT *

☐ * QUALIFIED
☐ * PROBABLY NOT

OTHER INSTRUCTIONS:
_____
_____
_____

73

Laundry, part 1: Washing

WHAT ARE YOUR RULES FOR DOING A LOAD OF LAUNDRY?

☐ DO A COIN AND TISSUES CHECK BEFORE WASHING*
☐ I HAVE NEITHER THE TIME NOR THE ENERGY TO CHECK SUCH THINGS

☐ FOLLOW CARE INSTRUCTIONS ON LABELS TO THE LETTER
☐ IF IT DOESN'T LOOK LIKE IT WILL FALL APART, IT GOES IN THE MACHINE
☐ SEPARATING WHITES AND COLOR IS GOOD ENOUGH FOR ME
☐ DELICATES MEANS HANDWASH, NOT SHOVING UNDERWEAR IN A
  PILLOWCASE FOR THE WASHING MACHINE TO DEAL WITH IT
☐ DELICATES MEANS SHOVE UNDERWEAR IN A PILLOWCASE FOR THE
  WASHING MACHINE TO DEAL WITH IT

☐ LIMESCALE REMOVER. BRAND:_____
☐ FABRIC SOFTENER. BRAND:_____
☐ DETERGENT. BRAND:_____

LIQUID // GEL // GEL POUCH THING // POWDER
// EXTRA SENSITIVE

*FINDERS KEEPERS POLICY, YOUR OWN FAULT FOR NOT CHECKING...
AND ALSO FOR NOT DOING YOUR OWN LAUNDRY

☐ I TAKE ALL MY CLOTHES TO THE
  DRY CLEANERS
☐ I GET_____TO TAKE
  MY CLOTHES TO THE DRY CLEANERS.
☐ DRY CLEANERS? WHAT AM I,
  A MILLIONAIRE? I BUY CLOTHES
  THAT DON'T NEED DRY CLEANING
☐ I'M NOT A MILLIONAIRE BUT I DO
  HAVE CLOTHES THAT NEED DRY
  CLEANING SOMETIMES

OTHER RULES:_____
_____
_____

Laundry, part 2: Line drying

HOW SHOULD CLOTHES BE HUNG OUT TO DRY? MARK YOUR PREFERRED STYLE

PANTS

SKIRTS

DRESSES

T-SHIRTS, SWEATERS

SHIRTS, BLOUSES, COATS

TOWELS, SHEETS

SHORTS, BOXERS, UNDERWEAR

SOCKS, TIGHTS

OTHER SCHOOLS OF THOUGHT:

Laundry, part 3: Tumble drying, ironing, folding

DRYING:
- [ ] THERE ARE SUCH THINGS AS AIR AND WIND. USE THOSE INSTEAD
- [ ] TUMBLE DRY WHEN NECESSARY
- [ ] TUMBLE DRY AS A NECESSITY
- [ ] ALWAYS CHECK THE CARE LABEL
- [ ] REMOVE THE LINT TRAY EVERY ONCE IN A WHILE

IRONING:
- [ ] FOLLOW CARE AND HEAT SETTING INSTRUCTIONS ON LABELS TO THE LETTER
- [ ] NO IRONING, IT'S GOING TO WRINKLE WHEN I WEAR IT ANYWAY
- [ ] BUY CLOTHES THAT DON'T NEED IRONING
- [ ] IRON JUST THE PARTS THAT WILL SHOW AND WEAR A SWEATER TO COVER THE REST
- [ ] YES, ACTUAL IRONING, NOT JUST STICKING IT UNDER THE MATTRESS OVERNIGHT AND HOPING FOR THE BEST

LAUNDRY SHOULD BE FOLDED:
- [ ] TO SALES-ASSISTANT STANDARD
- [ ] TO MILITARY STANDARD
- [ ] SHOWING A WORTHY ATTEMPT
- [ ] THAT'S NOT GOING TO HAPPEN

OTHER COMMENTS:
_____
_____
_____

Closet and laundry system

HOW ARE YOUR CLOTHES ORGANIZED?
- ☐ BY COLOR
- ☐ BY TYPE (E.G., PANTS, T-SHIRTS, SOCKS)
- ☐ BY SEASON AND TREND
- ☐ THEY AREN'T. I ONLY DISTINGUISH BETWEEN CLEAN / NOT CLEAN (A BALANCE BETWEEN SMELL AND WHETHER IT LOOKS CLEAN ENOUGH)

WHEN SHOULD CLOTHES BE WASHED?
- ☐ AFTER 1 DAY'S WEAR
- ☐ AFTER 2 DAYS' WEAR
- ☐ AFTER 3 DAYS' WEAR
- ☐ AFTER 4+ DAYS' WEAR (PLEASE SPECIFY:_____)
- ☐ WHEN THEY START TO SMELL
- ☐ WHEN THEY'RE VISIBLY DIRTY

OTHER NOTICES: _____
_____
_____

HOW OFTEN SHOULD SHEETS BE WASHED?
- ☐ EVERY DAY
- ☐ EVERY OTHER DAY
- ☐ EVERY FEW DAYS
- ☐ ONCE A WEEK
- ☐ LESS OFTEN THAN ONCE A WEEK (PLEASE SPECIFY:_____)
- ☐ WHEN THEY START TO SMELL
- ☐ WHEN THEY'RE VISIBLY DIRTY

HOW OFTEN SHOULD TOWELS BE WASHED?
- ☐ EVERY DAY
- ☐ EVERY OTHER DAY
- ☐ EVERY FEW DAYS
- ☐ ONCE A WEEK
- ☐ LESS OFTEN THAN ONCE A WEEK (PLEASE SPECIFY:_____)
- ☐ WHEN THEY START TO SMELL
- ☐ WHEN THEY'RE VISIBLY DIRTY

DO YOU HAVE A LAUNDRY DAY?
- ☐ NOPE
- ☐ YES, IT'S: _____

Keys to the kingdom

IF YOU FORGET YOUR KEYS, I WILL:
- ☐ WELCOME YOU BACK WITH A SMILE AND THE COINCIDENTAL AROMA OF FRESHLY BAKED COOKIES
- ☐ BEGRUDGINGLY LET YOU IN, MUTTERING ABOUT BEING IN THE MIDDLE OF SOMETHING, LIKE A GAME WHERE YOU CAN'T SAVE, OR HOW THE SPAGHETTI WILL NOW BE OVERCOOKED
- ☐ POINT AND LAUGH AT YOU THROUGH A WINDOW, LEAVING YOU TO PONDER YOUR OWN STUPIDITY ON THE DOORSTEP
- ☐ IGNORE YOU AND LEAVE YOU ON THE DOORSTEP
- ☐ LET YOU IN AS NORMAL, SO THAT YOU LET ME IN WHEN I FORGET MY KEYS, WHICH IS OFTEN

DO NOT:
- ☐ PUSH THE DOORBELL MORE THAN TWICE
- ☐ PUSH THE DOORBELL MORE THAN ONCE
- ☐ PUSH THE DOORBELL AT ALL—IT'S YOUR OWN FAULT FOR FORGETTING YOUR KEYS
- ☐ KNOCK REPEATEDLY OR ATTEMPT TO ATTRACT MY ATTENTION. I HEARD YOU. I JUST DON'T CARE
- ☐ TRY TO CLIMB THROUGH A WINDOW INSTEAD. YOU WILL SCARE THE LIFE OUT OF ME AND I MAY ACT RASHLY

IF YOU ARE INVITING PEOPLE OVER, GIVE ADVANCE NOTICE AND CHECK IT'S O.K:
- ☐ > ONE MONTH AHEAD
- ☐ ONE WEEK AHEAD
- ☐ A COUPLE OF DAYS AHEAD
- ☐ A COUPLE OF HOURS AHEAD
- ☐ WHENEVER, IT'S FINE WITH ME
- ☐ JUST SHOUT WHEN YOU COME IN

OTHER NOTES:
....
....

The art of war

HOW TO DEAL WITH NEIGHBORS, BURGLARS, AND THINGS THAT GO BUMP IN THE NIGHT

TYPE OF ENEMY:	PREFERRED METHOD FOR DEALING WITH SAID ENEMY:	WHO SHOULD DO IT:
ANNOYING NEIGHBORS	☐ STEAL THEIR MAIL ☐ SEVERED HORSE'S HEAD—THE HORSE DOES NOT HAVE TO BELONG TO THEM ☐ STRONGLY WORDED LETTER ☐ OTHER: _____	
BURGLARS	☐ MARTIAL ARTS ☐ USE OF BLUNT OBJECT BUT NOT VIOLENTLY ENOUGH TO GO TO PRISON, BECAUSE YOU WOULD NOT DO WELL IN PRISON ☐ CALL THE POLICE ☐ OTHER: _____	
MURDERERS / ASSASSINS	☐ SELF-DEFENCE SKILLS / MARTIAL ARTS ☐ USE OF BLUNT OBJECTS, SHARP OBJECTS, AND ANYTHING THAT CAN BE USED AS A WEAPON THAT HAPPENS TO BE NEAR TO YOU ☐ CALL FOR HELP, IF POSSIBLE ☐ OTHER: _____	
GHOSTS / THE SUPERNATURAL	☐ THERE'S NO SUCH THING AS GHOSTS AND THE SUPERNATURAL—ONLY SCIENCE ☐ USE EXORCISM TECHNIQUES ☐ CALL IN A PRIEST / PROFESSIONAL EXORCIST (NAME: _____) ☐ OTHER: _____	
OTHER		

Pony, cat or Komodo dragon?

PLEASE CHECK WHICH ANIMALS YOU WOULD BE FINE WITH KEEPING AS A PET.
DOUBLE-CHECK THE ONES YOU REALLY LIKE

DOMESTIC:
- [ ] CAT
- [ ] DOG
- [ ] HAMSTER
- [ ] MOUSE
- [ ] RAT
- [ ] RABBIT
- [ ] GUINEA PIG
- [ ] FERRET
- [ ] GOLDFISH
- [ ] PONY
- [ ] HORSE
- [ ] DONKEY
- [ ] TORTOISE
- [ ] PARAKEET
- [ ] CANARY
- [ ] PARROT
- [ ] SEA-MONKEYS
- [ ] OTHER: _____

EXOTIC:
- [ ] SNAKE
- [ ] MONKEY
- [ ] LIZARD, GECKO, IGUANA
- [ ] KOALA
- [ ] TIGER
- [ ] KOMODO DRAGON
- [ ] TARANTULA
- [ ] STICK INSECT
- [ ] OTHER: _____

SUPERVILLAIN:
- [ ] PIRANHAS
- [ ] SHARK
- [ ] JELLYFISH
- [ ] ANACONDA
- [ ] CHEETAH
- [ ] SIBERIAN TIGER
- [ ] CROCODILE
- [ ] OTHER: _____

THINGS TO REMEMBER:
_____
_____
_____

CARE INSTRUCTIONS:

IF YOU HAVE A HOUSEHOLD PET ALREADY, PLEASE STATE WHO IS
RESPONSIBLE FOR LOOKING AFTER IT

☐ IT'S YOUR PET, YOU LOOK AFTER IT
☐ IT'S OUR PET, WE'LL LOOK AFTER IT
☐ YOU CANNOT BE TRUSTED WITH A LIVING THING. NOT A CACTUS.
   NOT A GOLDFISH. I'LL LOOK AFTER IT

WHEN YOU GO AWAY, WHAT SHOULD HAPPEN TO YOUR PET?
☐ DESIGNATED PET-SITTER PERSON. NAME: _____
☐ DESIGNATED PET-SITTER PLACE. NAME: _____
☐ I'M TAKING IT WITH ME

OTHER NOTES:
_____
_____
_____

Things I can/cannot
deal with in the house

PLEASE MARK WITH A CHECK OR A CROSS

 ☐ SPIDERS (SMALL)
(CUP AND PAPER)

 ☐ SPIDERS (BIG)
(CUP AND PAPER)

 ☐ FLIES, MOSQUITOES, BEES, WASPS
(SHOOING OUT OF A WINDOW,
WELL- THWACKED NEWSPAPER)

 ☐ MICE, RATS
(EXTERMINATE)

 ☐ PIGEONS, SEAGULLS
(PIGEON- /SEAGULL-WHISPERING)

 ☐ SNAKES, BATS, CATERPILLARS,
BEETLES, SCORPIONS, COCKROACHES,
ALLIGATORS, GHOSTS, OTHER
(AS NECESSARY)

OTHER THOUGHTS:
_____
_____

Are you afraid of the big bad wolf?

WHAT ARE YOU AFRAID OF, OR WHAT PHOBIAS DO YOU HAVE?

- [ ] GHOSTS
- [ ] THE DARK
- [ ] HEIGHTS
- [ ] CLOWNS
- [ ] MONSTERS / THE UNDEAD
- [ ] THUNDER AND LIGHTNING
- [ ] CONFINED SPACES
- [ ] OPEN SPACES
- [ ] DOCTORS / ANYTHING MEDICAL
- [ ] GERMS
- [ ] OTHER: _____

OTHER COMMENTS:
_____
_____
_____

What's your kryptonite?

WHAT ARE YOU ALLERGIC TO?

- [ ] DUST
- [ ] POLLEN
- [ ] PERFUME
- [ ] SMOKE / INCENSE
- [ ] LATEX
- [ ] PENICILLIN
- [ ] CATS
- [ ] DOGS
- [ ] OTHER: _____

IS IT O.K. TO SMOKE IN THE HOUSE?

- [ ] YES, I'M A SMOKER
- [ ] YES, EVEN THOUGH I'M NOT A SMOKER
- [ ] NO, GO OUTSIDE

OTHER ISSUES:
_____
_____
_____

Preferred treatment when I am sick/have a cold

☐ CHICKEN SOUP
☐ HONEY AND LEMON
☐ MILD DRUGS
☐ STRONG DRUGS
☐ ICE CREAM
☐ NOTHING! LET ME BE!
☐ OTHER: _____

OTHER DEMANDS: _____
_____
_____

When I am upset...

☐ LEAVE ME ALONE
☐ MAKE ME A HOT DRINK
☐ GIVE ME A HUG
☐ TAKE ME OUT FOR A DRINK
☐ TAKE ME OUT
☐ HELP ME EAT MY FEELINGS
☐ OTHER: _____

AND RULES ON PERSONAL SPACE:
☐ I MUST HAVE SPACE, DON'T CROWD ME
☐ I AM A TOUCHY-FEELY PERSON
☐ SENTIMENT IN MODERATION

OTHER INSTRUCTIONS: _____

My legitimate indulgences on which you cannot judge me

☐ FOOD
☐ CLOTHES
☐ SATELLITE TV / BOX-SET BINGES
☐ SPORTS
☐ GAMES
☐ SHINY THINGS / COLLECTIBLES
☐ OTHER: _____

MY FAVORITE THINGS INCLUDE...

1) _____

2) _____

3) _____

4) _____

5) _____

OTHER NOTES:

IF YOU INSULT / DISLIKE THEM, WE CAN NO LONGER BE FRIENDS

The things we don't speak of under this roof

☐ RELIGION
☐ POLITICS
☐ FAMILY
☐ _____ (NAME OF SPORTS TEAM)
☐ OTHER: _____

MY PERSONAL POLITICS AND VIEWS (THINGS THAT
I STAND FOR):

1) _____

2) _____

3) _____

4) _____

5) _____

ADDITIONAL POINTS: _____
_____
_____

The bad habits that will drive me crazy

PLEASE LIST THE TRULY BAD HABITS YOU JUST CAN'T DEAL WITH, WHETHER IT'S PEOPLE NOT FLUSHING THE TOILET, DOUBLE-DIPPING IN SAUCES, LEAVING DIRTY SOCKS LYING AROUND, OR BITING THEIR NAILS. ADD YOUR OWN HERE:

1) _____

2) _____

3) _____

4) _____

5) _____

6) _____

7) _____

8) _____

9) _____

10) _____

OTHER COMMENTS / VIEWS:
_____
_____
_____

MY PERFECT DAY

MORNING

7 A.M. _____

8 A.M. _____

9 A.M. _____

10 A.M. _____

11 A.M. _____

AFTERNOON

12 NOON _____

1 P.M. _____

2 P.M. _____

3 P.M. _____

4 P.M. _____

5 P.M. _____

NIGHT OUT

6 P.M. _____

7 P.M. _____

8 P.M. _____

9 P.M. _____

10 P.M. _____

11 P.M. _____

12 MIDNIGHT _____

BEYOND MIDNIGHT _____

OTHER NOTES:

_____

_____

Event planning and going out

WHO GETS TO DECIDE WHAT TO DO AND WHERE TO GO?

* Rock, paper, scissors, flipping a coin or a duel are also effective methods for deciding between equally good options that everyone wouldn't mind doing—much better than endlessly debating, sighing and going "I don't mind" in circles.

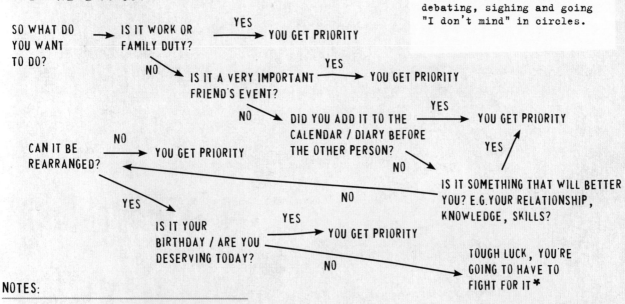

SO WHAT DO YOU WANT TO DO? → IS IT WORK OR FAMILY DUTY? — YES → YOU GET PRIORITY

IS IT WORK OR FAMILY DUTY? — NO → IS IT A VERY IMPORTANT FRIEND'S EVENT? — YES → YOU GET PRIORITY

IS IT A VERY IMPORTANT FRIEND'S EVENT? — NO → DID YOU ADD IT TO THE CALENDAR / DIARY BEFORE THE OTHER PERSON? — YES → YOU GET PRIORITY

DID YOU ADD IT TO THE CALENDAR / DIARY BEFORE THE OTHER PERSON? — NO → IS IT SOMETHING THAT WILL BETTER YOU? E.G. YOUR RELATIONSHIP, KNOWLEDGE, SKILLS? — YES → YOU GET PRIORITY

IS IT SOMETHING THAT WILL BETTER YOU? — NO → CAN IT BE REARRANGED?

CAN IT BE REARRANGED? — NO → YOU GET PRIORITY

CAN IT BE REARRANGED? — YES → IS IT YOUR BIRTHDAY / ARE YOU DESERVING TODAY? — YES → YOU GET PRIORITY

IS IT YOUR BIRTHDAY / ARE YOU DESERVING TODAY? — NO → TOUGH LUCK, YOU'RE GOING TO HAVE TO FIGHT FOR IT *

NOTES:
_____
_____
_____

All's fair in love and war

ON GAMESMANSHIP, SPORTSMANSHIP, AND RUINING FRIENDSHIPS

HOW SHOULD GAMES OF ANY SORT—BOARD, VIDEO, SPORT, OR LIFE—BE PLAYED?

- [ ] CHEATING IS ALLOWED
- [ ] CHEATING IS SO VERY NOT ALLOWED, NO EXCEPTIONS
- [ ] CHEATING IS ALLOWED AS LONG AS IT IS DONE CLEVERLY, VIA A LOOPHOLE OR IN A MANNER THAT MAKES EVERYONE SAY "FAIR ENOUGH"

- [ ] WINNERS MUST BE GRACIOUS
- [ ] WINNERS CAN BE AS CONDESCENDING AS THEY LIKE, SEEING AS THEY HAVE JUST PROVEN THEMSELVES TO BE BETTER THAN EVERYONE ELSE
- [ ] LOSERS MUST ADMIT DEFEAT WITH HONOR
- [ ] LOSERS CAN BE AS BEGRUDGING AND IN DENIAL AS THEY WISH, AS IS THEIR RIGHT

OTHER RULES:
_____
_____

- [ ] BATTLES MUST BE FOUGHT TOOTH AND NAIL, AFTER ALL YOU ARE YOU AND MUST BE RIGHT / THE BEST
- [ ] BATTLES MUST BE FOUGHT TOOTH AND NAIL, EVEN IF YOU KNOW YOU ARE WRONG / WILL DEFINITELY LOSE
- [ ] WINNING IS OVERRATED, AND FAR TOO MUCH EFFORT TO EVEN BOTHER ATTEMPTING
- [ ] A WIN IS A WIN IS A WIN, MY FRIEND, AND IT DOESN'T MATTER WHAT I DID TO GET IT
- [ ] PLAY FOR THE LOVE OF THE GAME, NOT TO WIN
- [ ] (DOES ANYONE ACTUALLY BELIEVE THAT LAST ONE?)

90

After a fight I will...

#%*!

- [ ] RETREAT TO ANOTHER ROOM, POSSIBLY CRYING
- [ ] STOMP ABOUT, BREAKING THINGS
- [ ] GIVE YOU THE SILENT TREATMENT
- [ ] RANT ALOUD TO MYSELF
- [ ] GO OUT FOR A WALK
- [ ] PACE AROUND THE ROOM
- [ ] RUN AWAY AND JOIN THE CIRCUS
- [ ] MAKE UP AND LAUGH ABOUT IT

SIDE NOTE: SWEARING

- [ ] I LOVE SWEARING, IT'S VERY THERAPEUTIC
- [ ] BAD LANGUAGE SHOULD BE USED LIKE PUNCTUATION, AND IS A VERY EFFECTIVE WAY OF CONVEYING EMOTION
- [ ] BAD LANGUAGE SHOULD BE USED SPARINGLY, SO AS NOT TO LESSEN ITS IMPACT
- [ ] SWEARING IS NOT PERMITTED—IT'S JUST PLAIN OFFENSIVE

COMMENTS: _____
_____
_____
_____

91

Hare or tortoise?

HOW GOOD IS YOUR TIMEKEEPING?

- ☐ ALWAYS EARLY
- ☐ RIGHT ON TIME
- ☐ FASHIONABLY LATE
- ☐ JUST PLAIN LATE
- ☐ A WIZARD ALWAYS ARRIVES EXACTLY WHEN HE MEANS TO

AND HOW DO YOU VIEW PEOPLE WHO ARE LATE?

- ☐ AS FELLOW LATECOMERS LIKE MYSELF
- ☐ I HATE PEOPLE WHO ARE LATE
- ☐ I DON'T REALLY CARE IF PEOPLE ARE LATE
- ☐ PEOPLE WHO ARE EARLY, ON TIME, OR EVEN FASHIONABLY LATE ARE OVEREAGER AND ACTUALLY WRONG, SO THERE

HOW FAST DO YOU LIVE LIFE?

- ☐ CHEETAH
- ☐ ROADRUNNER
- ☐ HARE
- ☐ WHERE'S THE FIRE? HUMAN IN A HURRY
- ☐ LORD / LADY OF LEISURE
- ☐ TORTOISE
- ☐ ZOMBIE TORTOISE
- ☐ DEAD TORTOISE

OTHER THOUGHTS:

_____

_____

_____

What do we celebrate?

- ☐ BIRTHDAYS
- ☐ ANNIVERSARIES
- ☐ CHRISTMAS
- ☐ VALENTINE'S DAY
- ☐ HALLOWEEN
- ☐ GUY FAWKES NIGHT

- ☐ STAR WARS DAY
- ☐ TALK LIKE A PIRATE DAY
- ☐ ANYTHING AND EVERYTHING, WILL LOOK FOR ANY EXCUSE E.G. HALF-YEAR BIRTHDAYS, FRIDAYS, TUESDAYS

OTHER HOLIDAYS:
_____
_____
_____
_____

Do we exchange presents?

☐ YES   ☐ NO

IF YES, WHAT IS THE MAXIMUM PRICE LIMIT?

- ☐ FREE / MINIMAL
- ☐ < $5
- ☐ $5–$10
- ☐ $10–$20
- ☐ $20–$50
- ☐ $50–$100
- ☐ $100+ (SPECIFICALLY: $_____)
- ☐ NO LIMIT

WHAT TO BUY ME
EXPENSIVE: _____
MODERATE: _____
CHEAP: _____

93

I've got your back if you ever...

- ☐ NEED A SECOND FOR A DUEL
- ☐ NEED MOUTH-TO-MOUTH RESUSCITATION
- ☐ NEED AN ALIBI
- ☐ OTHER: _____
_____

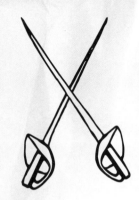

And in the event of apocalypse, know that...

- ☐ I HAVE PREPARED A BAG. IT'S HERE: _____
- ☐ MY WEAPON OF CHOICE IS: _____
- ☐ IF WE ARE SEPARATED, MEET ME HERE: _____
- ☐ I WILL SAVE YOU, AND ANYONE ELSE WHO NEEDS HELP
- ☐ I WILL SCREAM AND FAINT, AND BE OF NO USE WHATSOEVER
- ☐ I WILL BE COMPLETELY UNPREPARED
- ☐ YOU ARE ALLOWED TO EAT ME IF YOU REALLY MUST
- ☐ YOU ARE NOT ALLOWED TO EAT ME. DON'T EVEN THINK ABOUT IT

OTHER NOTES:
_____
_____
_____
_____

TEN COMMANDMENTS
of the house

LET IT BE WRITTEN THAT THE FOLLOWING RULES ARE
OF THE UTMOST IMPORTANCE AND MUST BE FOLLOWED:

1)

2)

3)

4)

5)

6)

7)

8)

9)

10)

SIGNED:

DATE:

ACKNOWLEDGMENTS AND STAFF CREDITS:

PUBLISHER SARAH FORD
ART DIRECTOR JONATHAN CHRISTIE
DESIGN EOGHAN O'BRIEN
SENIOR EDITOR ALEX STETTER
PRODUCTION CONTROLLER SARAH-JAYNE JOHNSON

ABOUT THE AUTHOR/ILLUSTRATOR:

FRANCESCA LEUNG'S FAVORITE THINGS ARE PIRATES, BATMAN®, AND CAKE, AND SHE SPENDS HER SPARE TIME PLAYING *ASSASSIN'S CREED*® OR LOSING AT MAHJONG. SHE MAKES THE BEST CUP OF TEA IN THE WORLD, ACCORDING TO HERSELF.

YOU WOULD NOT WANT TO LIVE WITH HER.